# Is it Rubbish?

Calling all aliens!

Are you planning a holiday to planet Earth?

**'Is it Rubbish?'**
**Published by MAVERICK ARTS PUBLISHING LTD**

Studio 11, City Business Centre, 6 Brighton Road,

Horsham, West Sussex, RH13 5BB, +44 (0)1403 256941

© Maverick Arts Publishing Limited August 2020


A CIP catalogue record for this book is available at the British Library.

## ISBN 978-1-84886-695-9

www.maverickbooks.co.uk

Credits:

**Finn & Zeek illustrations by Jake McDonald, Bright Illustration Agency**
Cover: Jake McDonald/Bright, Alf Manciagli /Shutterstock
Inside: **Shutterstock:** kostasgr (6 -7), Alf Manciagli (8), bensliman hassan (9), AePAR (10), Jag_cz (11), Darren Hugh Lynch (11), CC7 (12), Ilyashenko Oleksiy (13), Ko Thongtawat (14 - 15), SGr (16), Alba_alioth (17), Macrovector (18), AlenKadr (18), RecycleMan (19), iceink (19), GrumJum (20-21), Stor24 (22), Tatiana Zinchenko (22), Sergi Lopez Roig (23),luanateutzi (24), digieye (25), Africa Studio (25), beton studio (27)

This book is rated as: Orange Band (Guided Reading)
This story is mostly decodable at Letters and Sounds Phase 5.
Up to five non-decodable story words are included.

# Is it Rubbish?

## Contents

# INCOMING MESSAGE

Dear Finn and Zeek,

We want to visit Earth, but we don't want to leave any rubbish behind! Do humans recycle the things they use?

From Stitch and Soo
Planet Patch

# Introduction

The more people who live on planet Earth, the more rubbish they throw away. But who decides what is rubbish and what isn't?

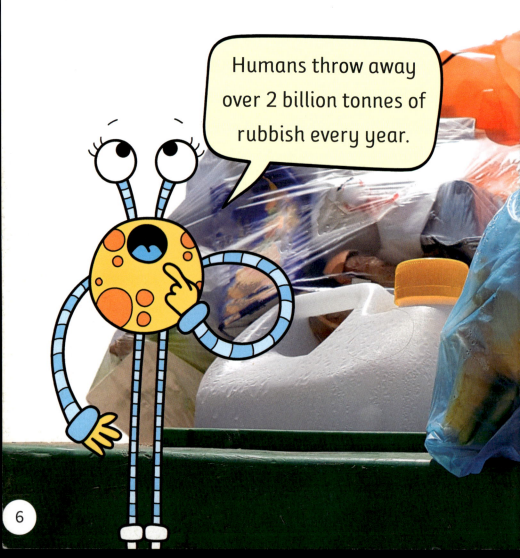

Humans throw away over 2 billion tonnes of rubbish every year.

If rubbish is left where it is, it can get very smelly. Fumes from rotting rubbish can make people ill.

To stop this from happening, rubbish is collected by special trucks and taken away. Sometimes rubbish is put in a giant hole called a landfill site. It can also be burned in an **incinerator**.

But the rubbish can still cause problems for humans! In the ground, rubbish can take a long time to **biodegrade**. Smoke from incinerators can **pollute** the air.

It can take up to 500 years for a baby's nappy to biodegrade!

The litter we drop ends up on streets, in fields and in the sea. It looks messy and can be dangerous. Humans could step on broken glass.

Mmm, yummy crisps. Now where's the bin?

Animals can also get caught in litter or eat it by mistake.

Factories and offices make a lot of rubbish. They must get rid of it safely – leaving litter behind is against the law!

A lot of rubbish can be recycled – this means turning it back into something useful.

Recycling is good for the planet. It stops rubbish dumps from filling up, and means less **energy** is needed to produce new things or burn old stuff.

Saving energy is a good idea, as it helps to prevent **global warming**. All sorts of things can be recycled. For example, old cardboard can be turned into hamster bedding!

Wow! So this empty box isn't rubbish after all.

How do you know whether something can be recycled? One way is to look for these three arrows. They mean: 'put me in the recycling bin, not the trash'!

When you put something in the recycling bin, what happens next? First, a lorry comes to empty the bin. The lorry takes the recycling to a **recycling plant.**

At this recycling plant, people are separating paper, plastic and cardboard so that they can be used again.

Plastics

Paper

Cardboard

Look how many plastic bottles have been collected at this recycling plant!

17

When everything is sorted, new things can be made. Broken glass can be washed, crushed and melted then made into new bottles or jars.

**FACT:** The energy saved by recycling <u>one can</u> of fizzy drink is enough to power a TV for <u>three hours</u>!

Clear plastic bottles can be turned into polyester, which is then used to make clothes. Yes, that's right – a lot of clothes are actually made from recycled plastic!

It took about nine plastic bottles to make this t-shirt!

Finding new ways to use stuff is really helpful for the planet. Try to ask yourself: "Is it rubbish, or can it be used again?"

Plastic bags, water bottles and takeaway containers can be used lots of times.

You can re-use or recycle things
in all sorts of ways.

Plastic
bottle

Car tyre

Plastic bottles can become bird feeders,
food waste can turn into garden **compost**,
and old tyres can be planters.

Making stuff from rubbish is fun. But always ask a grown-up to help you!

Grrrrr!

You can even turn toilet rolls into monsters!

Sometimes the easiest way to be kind to the planet is simply to use less stuff. In many parts of the world, people buy things they don't really need. There's so much in the shops it can be hard to resist! But in the end, all those extra things turn into rubbish.

## Plastic's Not Fantastic

Plastic can be recycled, but once it is finally thrown away it can take hundreds of years to biodegrade. If possible, buy things made from natural materials, such as cotton, wood, bamboo and wool.

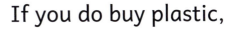

If you do buy plastic, try to re-use it, and be very careful never to leave any litter!

# MESSAGE SENT

Dear Stitch and Soo,

As you can see, people on planet Earth leave a lot of rubbish. But things that get thrown away can actually be very useful.

Make sure you look out for recycling bins when you visit. And try not to buy too much new stuff!

From,
Finn and Zeek x

Next time you need a toothbrush, try a bamboo one!

## Quiz

1. How many tonnes of rubbish do humans throw away every year?
a) 2 billion
b) 5 thousand
c) 3 million

2. What is the name of a place where rubbish is burned?
a) Dump
b) Landfill site
c) Incinerator

3. What does this sign mean?
a) Recycle me
b) Eat me
c) Wear me

4. Recycling means turning rubbish into something...
a) Tasty
b) Useful
c) Silly

5. How long can it take a nappy to biodegrade?
a) 500 years
b) 10 years
c) 12 weeks

6. Polyester is a type of...
a) Cotton
b) Food
c) Plastic

*Turn over for answers*

# Index/Glossary

**Biodegrade pg 9, 25**
This is when something breaks down into tiny pieces that will not harm the Earth. Light and air are needed to help things biodegrade. Water and the temperature can also help.

**Compost pg 22**
Garden compost can be made from things like old fruit and vegetable peelings, leaves, grass cuttings and egg shells. When these things are put together in a heap, they turn into a brown crumbly mixture that helps plants to grow.

**Energy pg 12, 13, 18**
Energy is what makes things go. Energy comes in lots of different forms, like heat, light and electricity.

**Global warming  pg 13**

The rising temperature of the Earth.

**Incinerator  pg 8, 9**

Where rubbish is burned at a very high temperature. The heat energy produced by an incinerator can be used to provide electric power.

**Pollute  pg 9**

To harm the environment with waste or chemicals.

**Recycling plant pg 15, 16, 17**

A place where rubbish is taken to be recycled.

# Book Bands for Guided Reading

The Institute of Education book banding system is a scale of colours that reflects the various levels of reading difficulty. The bands are assigned by taking into account the content, the language style, the layout and phonics. Word, phrase and sentence level work is also taken into consideration.

Maverick Early Readers are a bright, attractive range of books covering the pink to white bands. All of these books have been book banded for guided reading to the industry standard and edited by a leading educational consultant.

Fiction

Non-fiction

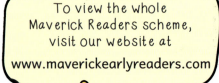

To view the whole Maverick Readers scheme, visit our website at www.maverickearlyreaders.com

Or scan the QR code above to view our scheme instantly!